copyright

MW01244150

ISBN: 978-0-9884316-6-2

forward

As a tech consultant who has studied human behavior for over 20 years, I have a deep understanding of how modern dating and apps work. Also, with 15 years of being single and going on over 500 first dates in that time, I've gained some priceless insight that I want to share with people who might be feeling overwhelmed at the idea of being single again.

I believe this book will be tremendously valuable for people who were in long term relationships for decades, and are facing the idea of re-entering today's complex dating landscape. My goal is to educate and empower you, so you can have proper expectations and make dating more of a pleasant adventure, and less of a nightmare.

I've been on every type of date imaginable. From being stuck in a desert at 2 a.m., to getting flown on a private jet to a celebrity party, I've seen it all and learned so much about human dynamics along the way.

I sincerely hope you find the insights here useful. My hope is this book will provide a useful guide that you refer back to and it helps you have a rewarding dating experience.

dedications

First I want to dedicate this book to everyone who is struggling with suddenly finding themselves single in the new world. I not only wrote this book for you, but because I know what it feels like personally, I want you to know that you aren't alone.

Also I want to thank all the people that gave me feedback including the ones I met dating and became great friends with. I'm also grateful for feedback from ex relationships who I could reflect back on with objectivity and wisdom.

A special thanks to Maureen. You provided so many great insights and ideas on the first draft including reading chapters from your phone in planes, trains, and automobiles and texting me feedback. Another great friend that came from online dating and inspired a lot of the writing.

Rhonda for also giving great feedback and keeping me honest! Also for sharing all of her experiences and being a great friend!

A special thanks to Allyson. You are not only one of the best editors I've ever worked with, but you've also been a great friend. You not only caught every little t that wasn't crossed, or i that was dotted, you shared your own harrowing stories along the way. Words cannot express how much you helped bring this to life.

table of contents

chapter one
introduction

If you find yourself single again after years away from the dating scene, brace yourself. The advent of dating apps and social media has radically transformed the landscape. What was once centered around chance meetings at bars, parties, or introductions to friends of friends, dating is now dominated by virtual connections.

This new environment can seem daunting. But approached with realistic expectations, openness to learn, and a spirit of fun, it can also be incredibly liberating. This book will be your guide to avoiding common pitfalls and increase your chances of having positive experiences.

For women especially, embracing safety precautions is non-negotiable. We'll cover ways to create online profiles that don't reveal too much personal information and discuss vetting potential dates through video chatting before meeting in person.

In the coming chapters, we'll explore topics like:

- The array of modern dating styles and choosing what fits your values
- Crafting an authentic and compelling online profile
- Navigating texting etiquette and digital communication norms
- Identifying red flags early without getting jaded

- Fostering physical and emotional intimacy at the right pace
- Recognizing when it's time to move on graciously

After being married, then single for the last 15 years, I've lived through the highs and lows of modern dating. I've also studied human behavior and technology for over 20 years. This book contains all of the wisdom I wish I had when I first rejoined the dating world after a long-term relationship.

Whether you're a baby boomer re-entering dating after divorce or the loss of a spouse, or simply someone who feels perplexed by the swipe-based dating culture, I hope the advice here provides you with knowledge, empowerment, and a little bit of fun.

Let's get started!

chapter two

how to know you're ready

Before diving back into dating, pump the brakes and evaluate your readiness. Attempting new relationships while still carrying pain and baggage from the past can taint your perceptions and derail potential connections.

It's like building a home. You wouldn't build something on an unstable foundation. Similarly, embracing new romance requires fortifying yourself first.

Rushing in while still wrestling with unresolved trauma, limited availability, or emotional turmoil turns dating into an uphill battle. You risk hurting yourself and others in the process. But taking time to address lingering wounds, gain self-awareness, and create space for new connections primes you for success.

Past Unresolved Trauma

Healing from relationship hurt takes time, especially if that pain stems from abuse, infidelity, neglect, or other betrayals of trust. When we experience these wounds, it's so tempting to guard ourselves by making sweeping judgments about "all men" or "all women." Our minds crave stories that explain away the hurt.

Sticking to rigid assumptions robs us of seeing each person as a fresh possibility. With support, we can dismantle these toxic narratives moving forward.

A friend of mine survived an abusive marriage, and for years after her divorce, she believed she was better off alone. Her ex-husband's cruel words had convinced her she was unworthy of real love. In therapy, she traced these beliefs back to childhood, when competitive siblings often teased her. She realized she had internalized lifelong messages that she was "less than."

This can have big effects on your perception of relationships.

Once she discovered this in therapy, she was able to control the narrative of her own value and started feeling confident that a better relationship was out there waiting. When we do the hard work of untangling pain from the past, we are less inclined to repeat it.

Unresolved pain also surfaces through intrusive thoughts. You meet someone exciting, only for nagging mental tapes to loop about how "no one stays" or "you'll just get hurt again." In therapy, you can learn skills to pause these thoughts and respond to what's real, not what haunts you from the past.

Understanding Love Languages

The concept of "love languages" offers insights into how we express and interpret affection. Introduced by Dr. Gary Chapman, in his popular 1992 book, <u>Five Love Languages</u>, here are some high level definitions.

Words of Affirmation - Some individuals feel most loved through verbal praise, encouragement, or gratitude. Hearing "I appreciate you" means the world. Share spoken appreciation often. This is something I personally respond to in a big way.

Acts of Service - For these people, actions speak louder than words. They feel cherished when you take on their chores, help with a project, project their needs, or offer practical support. This is definitely my personal jam. I love cooking for someone or doing little random things from time to time.

Receiving Gifts - Some appreciate the symbolic value of thoughtful gifts, cards, flowers, or other physical tokens. These represent care and time invested. Give little mementos that show you're thinking of them.

Quality Time - For these folks, full attention conveys love most deeply. Putting distractions aside to listen, having meaningful conversations, or sharing activities shows you care. Be fully present.

Physical Touch - Individuals who respond strongly to touch appreciate affectionate hugs, hand-holding, cuddling, or other physical closeness. Don't underestimate the power of human contact. Even the most subtle touching can be very powerful.

Keep in mind that we often use a blend of love languages. Discuss yours and your partner's primary dialects. Speaking in a way the other understands best will reinforce your mutual bond.

While the Love Languages model is widely popular, it's important to remember it's not scientifically proven. The categorizations are based on anecdotal observations rather than rigorous research. So view the languages as helpful frameworks, not definitive assessments.

The best way to determine which love language resonates with someone is to talk about it.

In reality, human relationships are highly complex. Some individuals strongly identify with a single primary love language. But many resonate with multiple languages, or see their preferences shift over time as partnerships evolve. Cultural differences also influence how people conceptualize and express love. Healthy relationships depend on much more than love languages, like trust, communication skills, and personal growth.

In summary, Chapman's concept can be a useful tool, but not the sole determinant of relationship success. Consider it one perspective among many others on the same topic, when nurturing your unique bond. Use love languages as a starting point for deeper understanding, while remembering that true connection exceeds any singular framework. Focus on cherishing your partner in a way that feels authentic to you both.

Attachment Styles

Attachment theory, rooted in the work of John Bowlby during the mid-20th century, describes the dynamics of long-term relationships between humans. Its most important tenet is that an infant needs to develop a relationship with at least one primary caregiver for social and emotional development to occur normally. As research grew, it was discovered that these attachment patterns established in childhood can continue into adulthood and play a role in our romantic relationships.

Here is my high level take of the the different types, and what the possible implications to dating are:

Secure Attachment:

Individuals with a secure attachment style feel comfortable with intimacy and independence, balancing them effectively. They often had caregivers who were responsive to their needs.

Implications for Dating: Securely attached individuals tend to have healthier, more balanced relationships. They're good at setting boundaries, can communicate their needs clearly, and don't harbor much fear about commitment or being alone.

Anxious Attachment (sometimes called preoccupied):

These individuals crave closeness and intimacy, are very attuned to their partner's actions, and tend to be insecure about the relationship. They may worry that their partner doesn't love or value them and seek constant reassurance.

Knowing I'm like this personally has somewhat helped me understand where the intrusive thoughts come from and how to prevent them from becoming outside dialogue.

Implications for Dating: Anxiously attached individuals may feel insecure when returning to the dating scene, constantly seeking reassurance and fearing rejection. They might rush into relationships or stay in unsatisfactory ones due to fear of being alone.

Avoidant Attachment (can be further subdivided into dismissive and fearful):

Those with an avoidant attachment style value their independence and often fear intimacy. They may keep you at a distance and use deactivating strategies to manage emotions.

Implications for Dating: After being in a long-term relationship, avoidant attached individuals might relish their newfound freedom, but may also find getting back into a dating scene challenging due to their fears of intimacy and commitment. They might avoid getting too close or bolt when things get too intimate.

Disorganized Attachment (also known as fearful-avoidant):

Individuals with a disorganized attachment style have a combination of anxious and avoidant tendencies. They desire close relationships but have significant trust issues and fear getting hurt.

Implications for Dating: Dating can be challenging for these individuals as they may find themselves drawn to relationships but deeply fearful of getting hurt. They might have tumultuous relationships or avoid dating altogether.

Attachment styles are patterns of behavior that dictate how we relate to our romantic partners. They are shaped by early childhood experiences and can significantly influence our approach to dating and relationships in adulthood.

Knowing one's attachment style can be beneficial when re-entering the dating world after a long-term relationship:

- It provides self-awareness, helping individuals understand their needs, fears, and behaviors in relationships.

- It offers insight into potential challenges one might face, such as anxieties, fears, or patterns of behavior.

- By recognizing one's attachment style, individuals can actively work on areas of growth, seek partners who complement or support their attachment needs, and strive for healthier relationship dynamics.

For someone returning to dating, it's essential to understand that while our attachment style can influence our relationships, it doesn't define them. Awareness is key. With understanding and effort, it's possible to work towards more secure attachments and fulfilling relationships. Also understanding someone else's attachment style can create a more objective perspective about how they operate.

If you want to learn more about attachment styles, this is where a therapist can really help.

Therapy

When you're carrying pain but longing for love, therapy is like hiring an objective coach to get you relationship-ready. Friends and family, as much as they care, have biases and agendas that can cloud their advice. A skilled therapist simply wants to equip you with the tools you need to thrive.

Because of my upbringing and how far I had come from that, I suffered from chronic imposter syndrome that I battled in every board room I've ever been in. This also led to a problem with dating that my therapist helped me recognize. She told me that my biggest issue with meeting someone, was that "my heart would fall in love with people that my head couldn't stand".

What it meant was that emotionally I felt safer with the type of people I grew up with, but intellectually, because of my completely different life experience as an adult, I no longer had that in common. This led to some reckless behavior that I eventually managed to curb dramatically.

Therapy can also help you identify self-defeating patterns you may not be aware of consciously. Do you sometimes sabotage relationships just as they start to flourish? Do you cling to incompatible partners out of fear? A professional can unravel why we self-protect in ways that become self-harm.

Below are 10 examples of dating issues to look out for that typically involve unresolved traumas:

1. Sabotaging a new promising relationship due to fear of getting hurt again. Pushing partners away or provoking conflicts right when things are going well.

2. Clinging to incompatible or abusive partners out of fear of being alone. Abandoning personal needs and making excuses for toxic behavior.

3. Hyper-vigilance and possessiveness. Needing constant check-ins or reassurance of fidelity due to past cheating or abandonment.

4. Avoiding vulnerability and emotional intimacy. Remaining closed off and distrustful of a partner's feelings and motives.

5. Projecting past hurts onto new partners. Judging everyone as guilty until proven trustworthy - seeing ghosts of exes instead of the real person.

6. Repressing anger and communicating passive aggressively instead of directly. Letting resentment build until it poisons the relationship.

7. Accepting disrespect or poor treatment. Having low self-worth and blurred personal boundaries.

8. Idealizing new partners initially. Looking past red flags and wanting the fantasy versus reality.

9. Repeating unhealthy attachment patterns. Choosing partners that validate self-destructive narratives.

10. Dating from a place of scarcity rather than abundance. Settling for anyone half-decent out of fear and loneliness.

Do You Have The Time And Focus?

Stepping back into the dating pool takes real commitment of time and mental energy. Like any garden, relationships require tending and care to grow.

So before downloading those apps, take stock of your current responsibilities and limitations. For instance, if your kids are young, your schedule revolves around their needs. Rushing into dating might leave you frustrated when last-minute cancellations happen.

I dated someone who had several teenagers and between that and her full time job, even seeing each other once a week was extremely challenging. There's certainly nothing wrong with that, of course, but you need to ask yourself that if you're in that position, and you like somebody a lot, how will you balance it?

Maybe demands at work leave you exhausted. Can you temporarily lessen commitments to create space for dating? If not, is now the season to prioritize your career over your love life? Listen to your needs.

For much of my career, I traveled extensively outside the US. Many of these trips were for extended periods up to three months at a time. Yet I would try to go on dating apps and meet people, only to be confronted with meeting someone I really liked, and then having to disappear for six weeks. I remember going on a date and having that chemistry with someone we all dream about, but then I had to go on several trips and there was no chance I was going to get a second date.

Eventually, I realized my lifestyle couldn't accommodate the consistency new relationships require. I had to make a choice between my professional demands and my desire for companionship. So I changed my career to be more available because my personal life suddenly became more important.

There are seasons for everything. If now isn't the time, don't force it. Focus on your personal growth, and when the timing aligns, you'll attract the right opportunities.

Some of the best advice I've ever received, is that the best way to spend time being single, is working on yourself. I went 6 months without meeting anyone I connected with. During that time I also decided to spend time at the fancy gym where I lived. As a result I adjusted my diet and lost 35 pounds. I now feel much better about myself, I have more confidence, and of course I'm much healthier!

chapter three
modern relationships

The dating landscape today hosts a diverse ecosystem of relationship models. Gone are the days of one-size-fits-all. Monogamy, situationships, open dynamics - there's a menu to suit various needs. But more options can also breed more confusion.

Firstly, don't let any stigma around "traditional" connections concern you. If an exclusive partnership resonates most, own it unapologetically. You deserve relationships on your own terms. Conversely, don't force yourself into modern configurations simply because they're trendy. Do what feels authentic.

That said, some flexibility serves you well. Needs and priorities evolve. While marriage was once the ultimate aspiration, today's singles frequently seek companionship without binding contracts. Many couples even start as friends with benefits before developing deeper care. Remain open and see where life leads.

Regarding age differences, judge not lest ye be judged. Yes, dating someone drastically older or younger draws some raised eyebrows. But focusing on chronological ages overlooks emotional maturity and life stage compatibility. An age gap relationship might raise questions, but those who dare to be different often thrive. More on the topic of age gaps later.

At the end of the day, the only "right choice" is the one that honors your core values while bringing mutual happiness, fulfillment, and respect. The configurations matter far less than the foundation beneath them. Define your own path.

What Are Some Modern Relationship Styles?

The styles below are examples of common relationship styles that work for some people, and not for others. It's important to make sure you're both on the same page when it gets to that point. It is also important to remember that even if it's not for you, try not to judge others just for being different.

Monogamy: This traditional model involves commitment to one exclusive partner. Monogamy provides intimacy and security for those who value loyalty. However, some struggle with long-term desire for just one person. Open communication about needs is key.

Situationships: Falling between dating and relationships, situationships involve intimacy without labels. This ambiguity offers freedom to let things unfold naturally. However, lack of defined expectations risks misunderstandings if both people aren't clear.

Friends with Benefits (FWB): A sexual relationship between friends without commitment. For those wanting physical intimacy without attachment, FWBs offer convenience. However, one person often develops unreciprocated feelings, causing pain. Strong platonic foundation, open and honest communication, and clear boundaries help.

Casual Dating: Dating multiple people without commitment. Casual dating allows fun and romance without pressure. For those desiring deeper emotional bonds, it may leave them unfulfilled long-term.

Open Relationships: A committed partnership with agreed upon sexual contact outside the primary relationship. This satisfies some people's desires for novelty and exploration. But jealousy may be too difficult for many monogamous-oriented individuals to overcome.

Polyamory: Consensual non-monogamy with multiple intimate partners. Polyamory rewards those able to do emotional work required, but is overwhelming for those wanting sexual/emotional exclusivity.

Slow Burn: Gradual relationship where intimacy unfolds slowly over time. Patience allows organic connection growth. However, slow pace can be frustrating for those desiring faster chemistry.

Whirlwind Romance: Rapidly progressing, passionate relationship. Whirlwinds satisfy cravings for excitement and intensity. But moving too fast risks burnout without first developing friendship. Just be sure this isn't the result of "love bombing" which is discussed later in the book.

Long Distance: Committed relationship where couples live separately. Provides autonomy while maintaining an intimate bond. But lack of cohabitation can strain emotional closeness over time. It can also make you feel lonelier than when you were single and dating depending on how frequently you see that person.

chapter four
single parents

Starting to date again after having kids introduces many additional considerations. The first is discussing the situation delicately with your ex-partner if you share custody. Have an open conversation about expectations and aim for positive co-parenting regardless of any disagreements. Also keep details about your private dating life discreet.

You'll also want to establish boundaries regarding introducing new partners to your children. Most experts say waiting up to 6 months before any direct contact is standard, but your comfort level and instincts should help guide you. From there, develop an incremental plan for contact that prioritizes your children's comfort levels over your excitement about the new partner.

Dating other single parents can seem ideal because they inherently understand your priorities and responsibilities better. However, don't force a connection solely due to shared parental status. Focus on your genuine chemistry and compatibility.

When talking to your kids, tailor discussions to their age level. For young children, provide basic context that you are going out with a new friend. With pre-teens, give a bit more detail but avoid oversharing romantic aspects. Emphasize that your love for them remains unchanged. Teenagers may need more direct points about sexuality and your evolving life.

Other key considerations include securing reliable childcare for dating nights and pacing yourself to avoid disrupting stability for your children. If a relationship progresses, carefully assess long-term compatibility regarding step-parenting.

Dating as a parent requires balancing your own needs with your children's adjustment. With a thoughtful approach and placing their wellbeing first, single parents can successfully navigate this new terrain.

If you don't have children, and you find yourself dating a single parent like I have in the past, just know that all of the above applies to you as well, so make sure you know what you're getting yourself into if you haven't had any parenting experience. I had a six year relationship and lived with her and her son. It was probably the closest, yet best exposures to parenting I've ever had.

chapter five
considering age

Age may just be a number, but in relationships, it can significantly influence expectations and compatibility. Traditionally, society frowns on large age gaps, but attitudes are shifting. Rather than chronological age, emotional maturity and life vision alignment matter most. In other words, sometimes a match made in heaven is when an old person meets someone younger with an old soul.

Still, generational differences exist. An older individual who married their high school sweetheart may be looking for a traditional courtship. A younger person accustomed to dating apps might view situations differently. Mismatched preferences around communication styles, relationship pacing, and boundaries can challenge creating connections.

Beyond values, pop culture references and sense of humor often reflect our formative years. A 50-year-old quoting Friends risks drawing blank stares from Gen Z dates. And shared laughter fortifies bonds. Finding the sweet spot takes some trial and error.

At the end of the day, an age-inclusive mindset serves us best. Unique combinations of youthful energy and seasoned wisdom can forge strong relationships. Dismissing potential partners solely based on age prevents discovering these rich connections.

Even when I was younger, I was always attracted to older women. However, what I learned in my own introspection was that it wasn't about being older, but I was more attracted to someone who had more wisdom or self confidence. By the time I was in my late 40s, I discovered that I had aged into what I was attracted to.

How Age Affects Dating

It is important to understand that different generations have different expectations, styles, and boundaries. Also if you are going to date someone who is generationally older or younger, it helps to understand these different generations' dating ethos.

Baby Boomers (born 1946-1964): This generation tends to prefer more traditional, long-term monogamous relationships leading to marriage. They are less likely to embrace modern styles like situationships or casual dating. Boomers value face-to-face communication over texting. They tend to prefer a slower relationship pace with traditional gender roles. Exclusivity and commitment are priorities when dating.

Generation X (born 1965-1980): Gen Xers are more open to modern relationship styles than Boomers, but still gravitate towards monogamy overall. They balance face-to-face interaction with digital communication. Gen X values emotional maturity and financial independence in partners.

They date with intention, seeking enduring companionship leading to settled families.

Millennials (born 1981-1996): Millennials are comfortable embracing modern relationship styles. They accept more fluidity in partnerships with a focus on finding fulfillment over labels. Texting is their primary communication method. Millennials date recreationally, keeping options open until finding "the one." Financial and emotional maturity still matter.

Generation Z (born 1997-2012): This generation is the most open to modern dating styles like situationships, polyamory and casual dating. Gen Z relies heavily on dating apps for making connections. They are explorative in relationships, focusing on youthful fun over serious commitment. Frequent text communication is preferred. Finding yourself is prioritized over finding forever partners.

While generalizations exist for each group, obviously there are exceptions. The keys are showing compassion for different values, communicating needs directly, and remembering healthy relationships take many forms.

Dating Someone Older or Younger

When you care for someone despite an age gap, the outside skepticism can sting, but society's judgments often reveal more about them than about you. With understanding and courage, you can face these challenges together and forge an unbreakable bond.

At first, scrutiny may come from those closest to you - family and friends who care but question the match based on age alone. Their caution likely comes from wanting to protect you. But they cannot see your lived experience, how this person stirs your spirit and nourishes your dreams. So listen to their concerns, then speak your truth. Share specific examples of your alignment and the joy you feel. Over time, your devotion can overcome their doubts.

I had tried dating someone once that was almost 15 years younger than me to try and be open minded. But I have to be honest, every time we went into a restaurant I could feel everyone staring and making assumptions about why were together. I wish I could say I rose above it, but I just hated that perception since it wasn't even close to being true and eventually I ended things.

Beyond judgment, practical differences arise too. Pop culture references may soar over each other's heads. Patience explaining teenage idols or old-school phrases, bridges these gaps with care. Discussing major historical events that shaped your perspectives also uncovers common ground. Recognize that you may need to translate each other's generational quirks at times.

With a large age gap, you may worry that energy levels, interests or mental sharpness don't fully align. However, some youthful spirits defy their age, just as some wise souls seem eternally young. Focus more on connecting emotionally and intellectually. Communicate your core aspirations in a relationship. If you uplift and energize each other, age fades away.

Gendered double standards also persist. Terms like "cougar" aimed at older women with younger partners seek to shame and ridicule. But don't let others' outdated views cloud a relationship. If you find true compatibility, seize it unapologetically. With secure self-esteem, compassion for outsiders' concerns, and meaningful conversation around needs and motivations, an age gap relationship can thrive. At the end of the day, only you two define your path.

Navigating an age gap takes courage and grace, but true love prevails. When you find someone who truly sees you, breathes joy into your days, and shares your vision for life's journey, any challenge can be conquered. Follow your heart boldly.

chapter six
online dating

How Online Dating Works

So you're ready to dip your toes into online dating. But before downloading any apps, let's walk through the typical process so you know what to expect.

At its core, online dating involves creating a profile showcasing your best self, usually with photos and a short bio. You indicate your preferences like location, age range, gender, and what you're seeking (casual dating, long-term relationship, etc).

The platform (website, mobile app, or both) presents you with profiles of potential matches based on compatibility. If you're interested, you take an action (e.g swiping right) indicating you like the profile and hopefully match if they like you back. If not, you ignore that profile (e.g. swipe left) to dismiss them. Mutual matches allow you to start chatting, either via text or an in-app messaging system. Each platform is slightly different and will be explained in more detail in the next section.

From there, you get to know each other online at whatever pace feels comfortable. You may move the conversation to text, phone, or video chat after establishing some rapport. Eventually, you may decide to meet up in person if you click over virtual communication. Be sure to read the section on Safety, Security, and Fake Profiles first.

While online dating opens up unprecedented access to connections, it isn't without its pitfalls. It can feel overwhelming, frustrating, and even dangerous at times if proper precautions aren't taken. But going in informed prepares you to maximize the positives while avoiding the negatives. The key is having realistic expectations and patience.

In the following sections, we'll explore how to choose the right platform for you, spot safety risks like fake profiles, verify someone's identity online, and handle common frustrations gracefully. I'll share tips so you can feel empowered taking your love life into the digital space.

Online Dating Safety

Navigating online dating calls for both excitement and diligence. With a few sensible precautions, you can uncover meaningful connections while steering clear of risky situations.

When chatting with a promising new match, it's tempting to dive into deep disclosures right away in your eagerness. Just hold back a bit on offering up your full name, workplace, or exact address early on. Just a few key details can be enough for someone to look you up directly. Build more rapport before providing specifics that allow you to be identified and located.

That said, basic intel like a first name and occupation can also work in your favor. Do some light vetting by searching social sites to confirm your match is who they claim to be. Just tread carefully and be somewhat thoughtful about people's privacy.

Before meeting someone face-to-face, thoroughly vet their identity. Search their name, photos, and phone number to uncover any questionable history or inconsistencies. Paid background check services like BeenVerified or TruthFinder offer added peace of mind.

If still unsure, use a disposable virtual number at first through apps like Google Voice. You can also use other alternative apps like WhatsApp, Google Chat, etc. to see what someone looks like before you even go to visit them. This helps with avoiding catfish surprises. It allows you to sever contact cleanly if needed. Whenever you do decide to meet in person, pick a public place like a popular restaurant or café during daytime hours. Informing friends and family of your plans provides another layer of protection, but sharing your location with them is even better.

Stay alert for any red flags suggesting a fake profile, like stilted English, dubious job titles, or repeated nudging to switch to texting off the app quickly. Reverse image search profile pictures to detect stolen photos. And verify any real social media presence beyond just a dating profile. One growing trend is many apps now have a verification process in which users take a selfie that is compared to their dating profile pictures. This has helped a lot. You can typically spot the little checkmark when someone is verified just like on social media.

Most importantly, listen to your instincts. Never feel pressured to meet someone if something feels amiss. You have every right to pause, delay, or end communication when situations give you concern or make you uncomfortable.

Dating online calls for care, but it shouldn't instill paranoia. With sound judgment, safety diligence, and a focus on reading people's character, you can uncover connections worth pursuing. Don't let a few bad seeds keep you from blossoming.

A friend shared a story about someone pretending to be in the US, but the app they were on showed he was 8,500 miles away. He of course blamed it on a glitch on the app, but after further discussions, it was clear he had created an entire identity on social media just to scam people. Be aware that scammers will probably know the app better than you, so if something doesn't sound right, do your homework.

Here are the top 5 most important safety tips to remember when online dating:

1. **Vet Before You Meet** - Always do a thorough background check on matches before agreeing to meet in person. Search their name, photos, number, etc. There are sites like mylife.com and even LinkedIn are good sources. Another suggestion is to do google image searches of the person's photos in their profile.

2. **Meet in Public First** - For initial meetups, choose a public place like a café or restaurant, especially during daytime hours.

3. **Inform Friends and Family** - Let loved ones know where you're going and who you're meeting, and set check-in times. Also allowing your people to track your location by phone is another great safety tip.

4. **Trust Your Instincts** - Don't feel pressured to move forward if something feels "off" - pause or end communications if needed.

5. **Guard Personal Details** - Be wary of sharing full name, employer, exact address early on until you've developed trust.

Understanding The Different Dating Platforms

Many platforms (website, mobile app, or both) are very similar, while others have a completely different model and style of how to meet people. After this section, I attempt to break down each of the platforms including some that are highly specialized.

It's important to note that these are descriptions based on researching the platform's website and reviews. I have also shared some of my personal experiences and thoughts for each platform listed, to share my perspective. It's also good to remember that these platforms are constantly shifting, and my descriptions and thoughts were based on experience up to the time of writing this book. Always do your homework before you sign up with any of them.

How To Pick The Right Platform

Navigating the myriad of options for online dating platforms can feel daunting. With so many apps and sites out there, how do you even begin to pick the right one for your needs?

First, consider starting with just one app initially, especially if you're a woman. The influx of matches and messages on some platforms can start to feel overwhelming. Juggling multiple options from the get-go runs the risk of inundation.

Before joining any platform, thoroughly research what sets each one apart. Get to know the target audience, unique features and user experience. You want to understand what makes this space the best fit for someone like you, whether it's the streamlined profiles, personality matching or specific community.

Also talk to your single friends, and ask them what they have used and what they liked or disliked about it. Even if you don't have a lot of single friends in your immediate circle, your friends probably have friends they can ask.

Always test drive the free version of a dating app before committing to a paid subscription. This gives you a chance to get acclimated and decide if the investment is warranted. Speaking of costs, those premium tiers can range anywhere from $10-30+ a month on average, with some escalating to the hundreds per month. Make sure the pricing aligns with your budget.

Be intentional about choosing an app that caters to what you genuinely seek, such as casual encounters versus serious relationship material. Don't overwhelm yourself by venturing too far outside your comfort zone initially. Ease into the experience.

Don't forget to read up on recent comparative reviews. Dating platforms rapidly evolve, so it helps to get the most current user impressions rather than outdated experiences. Also take time to understand the privacy policies and terms of use — you want to ensure your personal data is handled ethically.

Lastly, determine whether you prefer an app-only experience or one that also has desktop and website access. This choice comes down to personal comfort.

By carefully evaluating and selecting the right dating platform for your needs, you set yourself up for success. You can always expand your options later. You want to approach matchmaking with intention, not chaos.

Below are two different lists of dating apps. The General Dating platforms are mostly designed for the general public, where the Specialty platforms focus on niche areas of focus like lifestyle, age, or status. Many offer apps in addition to websites, where some only offer apps.

General Dating Platforms

The following are some popular dating platforms that I have either researched, had personal experience with, or both. Of course everyone has a different experience, this is just through my personal lens. For something more specialized, see the list after this.

Bumble

bumble.com

Bumble sets itself apart by having women initiate conversations after matching. Overall it attracts relationship-minded singles. Bumble is known for being female-empowered. Users join by making a profile and indicating dating preferences. Like Tinder, the paid model gives you a preview of who liked you first.

Pros: Female-led approach, quality over quantity interactions

Cons: Time limits for messaging, and smaller user pool. Some traditional women don't like sending the first message.

Personal Experience: Bumble adds an extra step of having women initiate messaging after matching, which I've found problematic. The majority of my matches expire without sending a message due to this deadline pressure. While Bumble may evolve this approach, as a researcher and student of human behavior, it seems this system discourages rather than encourages communication.

That said, some women I've met on the platform also shared disliking that initial pressure. Despite this hurdle, I've made great connections on Bumble, so an open mind can uncover rewards even when navigating certain friction points in the matching process.

Coffee Meets Bagel

coffeemeetsbagel.com

CMB provides curated matches and incentives to chat. It has a reputation as a female-friendly app that focuses more on quality over quantity of matches. Users join and get matched with a limited number of curated suggestions per day. At this time, the focus is searching for serious relationships.

Pros: High-intent users

Cons: Limited daily matches may slow the process

Personal Experience: I have not been on this platform in a long time. I think it was fine when I was on it, but I never really connected with anyone there, so I never returned.

eHarmony

eharmony.com

eHarmony focuses on lengthy compatibility questionnaires. The focus appears to be for commitment-minded singles looking for long-term relationships. eHarmony is known for attracting marriage-minded singles given its emphasis on lengthy compatibility tests during signup.

Pros: In-depth matching process, high-intent users

Cons: Lengthy signup, limited same-sex matching options

Personal Experience: I've never actually been on eHarmony, because I always felt like it wasn't for me. The description above was based on looking at their website and reading some reviews. So take this all with a grain of salt. I think it works great for people, but my impression was it's more geared towards people who are looking for more traditional relationships.

Facebook Dating

facebook.com/dating

Facebook Dating allows you to match with friends of friends while providing safeguards to protect your privacy. As part of the social media giant, Facebook Dating allows leveraging your existing connections and network for matches. Users opt-in by creating a dating profile separated from their main Facebook account.

Pros: Integration with existing Facebook network

Cons: Privacy concerns, less robust than standalone apps

Personal Experience: I have a neutral feeling about this. I have tried it twice. The first time didn't net me anything, but the second time I met someone who was really nice and still a good friend today. In my opinion, it's too broad of a community and doesn't feel like it has a theme or a focus, so it can feel overwhelming.

Hinge

hinge.co

Hinge matches you based on shared interests and common connections. Profiles focus on personality and prompts. Hinge has a reputation as the "relationship app" for its focus on profiles showing personality over just photos. It uses a combination of pictures combined with answers to standard questions to help you communicate your personality Users can join by linking their Facebook account and completing their profile.

Pros: High-intent users, personal profile focus

Cons: Potentially limited user base based on connections

Personal Experience: I've had pretty good luck on Hinge. Their unique approach to adding the questions and answers mixed with photos is a refreshing twist on the doom swiping where it becomes a thoughtless race to the bottom. I met the almost love of my life on Hinge so I'm a fan.

Match

match.com

One of the first dating sites, Match has decades of experience in algorithm-based matching and features in-depth profiles. Match is known for attracting serious, relationship-oriented daters given its robust matching system. Users join by making a detailed profile and subscribing to a paid membership.

Pros: Ideal for serious daters, robust matching algorithms

Cons: Costs money, older demographics

Personal experience: Match was the first website I joined after my divorce in 2008. It was a good experience in that I met someone, even though they lived way down the coast from me. It was very tough taking that first step, but doing so helped me get out of my own head and back out there meeting people.

I haven't been on Match in a while. I had a bad experience trying to cancel my membership with them the last time that left me not wanting to return. That was my personal experience, but others probably feel differently.

OkCupid

okcupid.com

OkCupid uses thousands of questions to determine compatibility percentages between users. Quirky and laid-back vibe. OkCupid has a reputation for being math-focused and using questionnaires to find personality matches. Users join by making a profile and answering optional compatibility questions.

Pros: Personality matching, globally popular

Cons: Imperfect matching algorithms, silliness can attract some insincere users

Personal Experience: I haven't been on this platform in a while. I had a similar experience where when I tried to get off, there was a significant challenge which always creates trust issues for me. I would say that I definitely met more interesting and creative types of people on OK Cupid, but no actual love connections.

Plenty of Fish

pof.com

One of the largest global dating sites with over 150 million users. Offers extensive filtering options for finding the perfect match. POF is known for having a robust user base and search filters to help users find their ideal partner. Users join by creating a profile with details, photos, and match preferences.

Pros: Active community with lots of choices, basic features free

Cons: Dated interface, high volume of inactive accounts

Personal Experience: Although I've tried it several times in the past, I've never had a connection there. I didn't really have a lot in common with people, and I know it has a reputation that's worthy of research.

Tinder

tinder.com

Tinder is one of the most used dating apps with millions of active users. Known for popularizing the "swipe" matching system, it prioritizes quick connections based mostly on photos. Tinder has a reputation for casual dating and hookups. Users join by creating a profile with photos, basic details, and preferences that others view and swipe on. The paid model includes letting you see who liked you first.

Pros: Large user base, easy signup, simple swiping system

Cons: Emphasis on looks over depth, many users not serious about dating. Constantly trying to get you to upgrade.

Personal experience: I would say I've met the most fun people on Tinder. I also had a couple of longer term relationships that started from that app. The most ironic thing I see is people acknowledging they are on an app known for hooking up, but stating they aren't looking for a hookup. Kind of like walking into a strip bar for a drink and stating loudly you aren't there to see naked people.

Specialized Dating Platforms

The following dating apps tend to be more niche and focused on specific interests.

Adult Friend Finder

aff.com

Adult Friend Finder is an adult-oriented dating and hookup site known for its sexually explicit content and user base looking for casual sexual encounters.

AFF has a reputation as one of the largest hookup and casual sex sites, with extensive nude photos/videos, live streams, chat rooms, etc. Users join by making a profile showcasing their sexual interests and preferences.

Pros: Caters to an adult demographic seeking casual sexual encounters

Cons: Explicit content and focus on sex may not appeal to those seeking meaningful connections

Personal Experience: I tried this platform off and on mostly out of curiosity. It's a great place to explore and meet people that are open minded and share common interests. The design is pretty dated, but it has a big population. Just be ready for lots of nudity and unique personalities.

EliteSingles

elitesingles.com

EliteSingles is a dating site aimed at educated and ambitious singles seeking long-term relationships.

It has a reputation for attracting commitment-minded professionals based on its selective membership, personality-based matching, and focus on compatibility. Users complete an in-depth signup process with a personality test.

Pros: Intelligent and motivated user base, thorough matching process

Cons: Lengthy signup, monthly fee for full access

Personal Experience: I have not personally used Elitesingles but in researching it, the selective and niche community seems appealing for career-oriented singles searching for serious connections. However, the membership fee may deter more casual daters.

Feeld

feeld.com

Feeld is an open-minded dating app aimed at explorative singles and couples interested in kink, polyamory, and alternative relationship styles.

Feeld has a reputation as one of the few mainstream dating apps welcoming of non-monogamous, LGBTQ, and kink-oriented users. Users join by creating a profile focused on desires, interests, and preferred relationship configurations.

Pros: Inclusive environment, focused on open-minded individuals

Cons: Smaller user base, privacy concerns around sexual preferences

Personal Experience: I have tried this app and did meet someone I had a non-traditional relationship with and we're still friends to this day. Honestly if you're in the market for something non-traditional, this feels like a pretty great app.

The League

theleague.com

The League aims to attract accomplished, ambitious, and busy singles by screening users and offering curated matches. Users apply by creating an in-depth profile, and admission is selective.

Pros: Career-focused community, strong screening process

Cons: Long waitlist, potential elitism or superficiality

Personal Experience: I've probably been on this platform consistently for the longest of any platform. I have paused my account many times, but because getting back in can take time, I've never actually closed it. I would say that for me, I've seen and met some of the most impressive people on a dating app including some celebrities.

I did have the paid version for awhile where you could see more than 3 a day and who liked you first, but I like the slow trickle. It's way less stressful and "doom scrolly" and because I tend to have more in common with who I see, the quality of potential matches has always been good.

Ourtime

ourtime.com

Ourtime is an over 50 dating site tailored specifically to mature singles looking for relationships and companionship.

Ourtime has a reputation as the go-to app for divorced, widowed or older adults starting to date again later in life. It focuses on pairing people with shared life experiences and values. Users create a profile and browse potential matches.

Pros: Large user base of mature singles, caters to older demographics

Cons: May lack some features and modern style of newer apps

Personal Experience: I have not used Ourtime but it seems like a good option for people over 40, especially those reentering dating after divorce or loss of a spouse. The ability to connect with others going through similar life changes could be very beneficial.

Raya

raya.com

Raya is an exclusive, members only dating app aimed at celebrities and creatives. It has a thorough application process. Raya has a high-profile reputation for catering only to elite influencers, models, artists and tastemakers. Users apply and must be referred by current members or Raya members.

Pros: High-profile network, strict entry standards

Cons: Very difficult to get invited, focuses on status

Personal Experience: I've been on the waiting list for almost a year at the time I wrote this. I'm not really sure if it's for me, but of course I'm curious!

Frustration and Disappointments

Online dating brings endless possibilities, but also its share of letdowns. I remember the deflated feeling when my witty openers got lost in an inbox avalanche, or the sting of excitement fading after yet another ghosting.

The sheer volume of options paradoxically makes selection overwhelming. Juggling conversations with multiple matches felt like spinning too many plates. Deception, however minor, always risks hurt when discovered.

In these moments of frustration, it helps to take a step back and regroup. Remind yourself that the right connections make the disappointments fleeting. There are kind, genuine people amidst the noise.

Focus energy on those who engage you sincerely, even if fewer and further between. Don't take ghosting or mixed signals personally. Each "no" gets you closer to your "yes."

It's okay to limit the playing field when needed. Prioritizing quality conversations preserves your time and attention for promising prospects. Give yourself permission to slow down.

While valid frustrations exist, you can mitigate them before they spiral. Be honest when expressing boundaries and take breaks when feeling overwhelmed.

Approach online dating as you do life - with patience, wisdom and optimism. The bumps along the way only help you cherish the beauty. In time, past hurts fade and new adventures shine brighter.

So breathe deep and brace yourself for the rollercoaster, but don't clamp down or retreat into cynicism either. The vulnerabilities that open you up to disappointment also allow you to find the joy.

chapter seven
creating a dating profile

When creating your profile, resist the urge to be someone you're not. I know, you want to cast a wide net and get lots of intriguing matches. But attracting people under false pretenses leads nowhere positive. Stay true to you - trust me, your spirit will shine through and draw the right connections.

Yes, leading with your boldest, most clever self may garner initial attention. However, those drawn in by superficial traits will eventually be disappointed by the real you. Don't waste time. Better to let a few less sparks fly and wait for someone who cherishes your essence.

The more you filter, enhance, exaggerate or conceal, the further you drift from your harbor, where kindred ships await. Remain anchored in authenticity. Share your hopes, showcase your hobbies, reveal your quirks. The right people will be drawn to you naturally.

Staying grounded in self-assuredness and patience allows love to find you in proper time. Don't lose heart! When you lead boldly as your authentic self, the matches that matter will take notice.

The following are the five ways to get started on creating the right profile for you.

Step 1: Pick The Platform That's Right For You

Different platforms have different ways of structuring and displaying your profile. For some it's as easy as adding a few pictures, checking a few boxes about age and location and you're ready to go. For others it's as complicated as creating a Facebook profile including extended statistics and surveys.

Figure out which one makes the most sense, and then understand what that platform requires, and even research what some of the best strategies are for that platform depending on your goals.

Step 2: Curate Your Photos

Your photos are probably one of the most important things on your dating platform. With the popularity of video on social media, it's also making its way into dating apps as well. Like it or not, people have become accustomed to swiping without even looking at your bio so this is your most important chance to catch the attention of your best matches.

The following is a list of Do's and Don'ts when getting your photos ready:

Do's:

- Have 5-7 photos ready that showcase your interests and personality

- Include a clear headshot and a full body shot

- Learn to use the camera timer on your phone so you have time to pose away from the camera

- Show your authentic, unfiltered self

- Use recent photos from the last 1-2 years

- Include fun activity/hobby pics that highlight your passions

- Get feedback from objective friends on the best shots

- Lead with your most genuine appealing photo

- Mix close-ups and full body pics to build intrigue

- Show mentioned pets in bio

- Try to include some pics with friends to show your social side

- If you normally don't wear a lot of makeup, then be sure to include some of those pics as well

Don'ts:

- Heavily filter or edit photos to misrepresent your appearance

- Use photos with redacted exes or people who are unrecognizable

- Include pics that reveal where you live/work if privacy is a concern

- Pick the same theme or background for all your shots

- Men: Shirtless gym selfies or hunting photos if they don't appeal to your target audience

- Women: Duck lips, excessive cleavage shots, overly sexy poses if they don't match your intentions

- Pics that are 10+ years old if you look significantly different now

- Bathroom mirror selfies or sloppy backgrounds

- Anything that feels inauthentic to how you want to present yourself

- It's probably not a good idea to show pictures of young kids for safety reasons

Step 3: Your Written Bio

Your bio is far more than just a supporting actor in your online dating profile. Consider it the leading lady or man — your opportunity to let your essence shine through with humor and heart. While photos may draw initial interest, words seal the deal, conveying the spirit behind those pretty pictures. An engaging, well-crafted bio transforms you from just another charming face to someone with depth, interests, and intrigue.

It brings your story to life, makes common connections click, and sparks conversation. So don't shortchange your profile by skimping on the bio. Let it capture your unique perspectives, passions, and personality with authenticity. This is your chance to express who you really are so your kindred spirits can find you.

The lists below are some do's and don'ts to consider when writing your bio:

Do's:

- Know the character limit of your chosen platform
- Write conversationally in your authentic voice
- Share your passions, dreams, interests, and quirks
- Sprinkle in humor and warmth if it reflects your personality

- Include unique facts, opinions, and anecdotes

- Ask thoughtful questions to spark dialogue

- Showcase your spirit and what makes you you

- Let AI tools help you summarize key points so it's still authentic, but with a virtual writing coach

- Have trusted friends review to get feedback

- Research platform norms for ideal bio length

Don'ts:

- Leave your bio empty or barely filled out

- Use cliches or generic, broad statements

- Bash exes or air emotional baggage

- Use offensive language or touchy topics

- Make sweeping generalizations about groups

- Simply list basic stats and facts

- Hide your true personality and interests

- Write idealized perfection; embrace quirks!

- Go way over or under recommended word count

- Forget to tailor bio to the specific audience

- Hesitate to rewrite and refine over time

Step 4: Extended Bio and Platform Surveys

Many dating platforms like OK Cupid, Match, and eHarmony rely on compatibility questionnaires and stats to match you with aligned singles. When filling these out, answer thoughtfully and honestly to get the most accurate results. Other apps simply have you indicate basic info like height, religion, politics, and lifestyle to filter.

Take time to provide accurate relationship goals, personality type, and interest data. The more meticulous you are, the better the algorithm can connect you with those on the same wavelength. But don't treat it like a resume listing achievements. Be real about flaws, quirks, and those love-it-or-hate-it passions of yours. And don't worry, your answers aren't set in stone. You can revisit and update your stats as you grow and evolve. The right matches for who you are now await discovery!

A note about religion and politics: Politics have become such a polarizing issue that many times people do not want to see or connect with people unless they are in a specific political party. This can be true of some religions as well.

Because I now live in Arizona, but came from California, I've had people make wild assumptions about me and even get angry when they found out where I was from!

So to avoid anything that might create unnecessary attention or potential conflicts, it's better to be open. Keep in mind there's the occasional person who thinks they can change you, and let me just apologize on their behalf now.

Step 5: Don't Be Afraid To Make Changes

Just like you grow and change, don't be afraid to rework your dating profile to align with who you are now. For example, if a trusted friend feels your current bio isn't highlighting your true spirit, take their feedback to heart. Revise what isn't ringing authentic and see if you start attracting more compatible matches.

Or maybe you've adopted a new furry friend recently that you really want to showcase. Adding a photo highlighting your latest canine or feline companion not only updates your profile, but also lets animal lovers know you're one of them!

Life circumstances, passions, and even dating preferences evolve. If you've made a career change, share that new vision. If salsa dancing has become your latest craze, paint a picture of your new hobby for others to ask about. And if you find you're now seeking long-term compatibility over casual fun, rework your bio to specifically attract those relationship-minded individuals.

Revisiting your dating profile keeps it current, genuine, and optimized to manifest connections that nourish you now. Don't let stagnancy lead to missed opportunities. By putting your latest, greatest self out there, you just may discover fresh matches better suited for your growth.

chapter eight

making connections

Online dating profiles offer clues into someone's personality, values and communication style if you look closely. But don't get overly caught up in projections based on photos and captions alone. Profile chemistry doesn't always align with in-person chemistry. Balance curiosity with reasonable expectations.

The paradox of choice is real. Endless profile swiping and messaging options leads some to constantly second guess selections and experience fatigue. Stay focused on quality connections that energize you rather than collecting matches or seeking perfection.

Watch for **red flags** suggesting serious incompatibility:

- Intolerant religious/political views
- Disrespectful or dismissive of service workers
- Calling exes "crazy" or talking about them too much
- Arrogance, negativity, anger issues
- Overly aggressive
- Rigid demands around gender roles
- Suspicious questioning early on or other controlling signs
- Lazy communication or frequent delays responding

- Love bombing where someone showers you with affection way too soon and tries to move things too fast (see below for more details)

Seek out these positive **green flags**:

- Thoughtful and open communication
- Emotional maturity and self-awareness
- Knows how to read the room
- Respectful
- Shared priorities, values, and interests
- Engaging questions and humor
- Consistent enthusiasm and availability
- Reciprocating interest

Trust your instincts when evaluating matches - does conversing feel easy and enjoyable? Don't force connections that don't align with your authentic self.

Fail fast and politely end contact with clear mismatches early. Rejection brings you closer to individuals you resonate with.

Love Bombing

Love bombing refers to showering someone with over-the-top affection and promises of commitment very early in the relationship. The excessive gifts, compliments, and attention make the recipient feel incredibly special at first. However, it often stems from harmful motivations.

The psychology behind love bombing relates to narcissism and manipulation. Bombers use these tactics to control a partner by eliciting emotional dependence. Their self-esteem relies on this power imbalance. It also frequently correlates to issues like attachment disorders or childhood trauma.

The pitfalls become evident when bombers abruptly withdraw the affection as quickly as it started. This drastic shift leaves recipients confused, devastated, and missing all of the attention. Bombers then use this manipulation to keep partners chasing them.

Being the target of love bombing can be incredibly seductive at first. Who doesn't enjoy feeling like the most important person in someone's world? But eventually the constant praise and premature commitment feels smothering. Healthy relationships build steadily, not through unrealistic idealization.

When bombers sense the recipient pulling back, they withdraw all attention. This denial is intended to bring the target back under their control through emotional starvation. The rocky foundation then crumbles.

If you suspect you're being love bombed, don't ignore red flags just because the attention feels good. Focus on their actions, not just their words. Ask for reasonable pacing. Watch for other manipulative signs and don't relinquish your independence. Remain grounded in your self-worth.

If I had to be honest, I've been on both sides of this dilemma. I've met people who I was convinced they were "the one" and then I was too open about how I was feeling because I was so excited. I'm not saying that was the sole reason it ended, but it certainly didn't help matters.

On the contrary, I've also been the recipient of love bombing and it can feel like you're in a very fast moving storm that is hard to keep up with. It can feel overwhelming and rush something that might have been fine if it had the proper amount of time to develop.

Final Words on Online Dating

Studies show men initiate more matches online but receive fewer responses than women. But quality connections depend on mutual effort. Patience and perseverance pay off.

With realistic expectations, staying true to yourself, and maintaining healthy boundaries, online dating can unlock exciting new relationships.

chapter nine
getting help

If navigating the world of online dating isn't for you, then getting the help of a professional can be a great investment. Many can connect you with people who are like minded and share the same values. There are two kinds of help you can enlist; dating coaches that act like advisors, and matchmakers who actually help you connect with people in their network.

Dating Coaches

Dating coaches provide personalized guidance to help you succeed in modern romance. Through tailored advice and feedback, they support you in improving your dating skills, identifying relationship needs, crafting compelling profiles, and boosting confidence.

A key benefit of working with a dating coach is gaining insights from an objective outside perspective. Friends may try to help but lack impartiality. Coaches analyze experiences and patterns to offer you sage advice. You also receive ongoing support navigating the gamut of modern dynamics from apps to ghosting.

To find a qualified dating coach, ask for referrals from friends or well-established matchmaking companies. You can also search on Google or even on the different social media platforms. One trick is to search hashtags like #datingcoach to discover and get to know them before you even reach out.

Vet credentials like psychology licenses, matchmaking certifications, or relationship science expertise. Also consider specialty areas that align with your needs.

Choosing the right coach fit involves knowing your specific goals, values, and personality. Do trial sessions to get a feel for coaching styles and rapport. An encouraging yet honest coach who instills optimism will serve you best. Discuss details like pricing, availability, and the coach's own relationship background.

A key difference from matchmakers is that dating coaches advise you on achieving success versus acting as a liaison. You retain control over meeting new people. Their guidance helps you flourish organically. Matchmakers introduce you to compatible singles. So coaching benefits singles at all stages - not just those ready for serious commitment.

The right dating coach empowers you to embrace dating with self-assurance. Their wisdom guides you down your personalized path to romantic fulfillment.

Matchmakers

Matchmakers provide a more hands-on approach to finding love compared to impersonal dating apps. But how do they work, and could hiring one benefit you?

Matchmakers come in two forms - independent operators, or those aligned with a larger matchmaking company. Their incentive is fairly consistent however - facilitating successful matches to earn fees and gain referrals.

The process generally involves extensively interviewing clients about their relationship goals, ideal partner attributes, lifestyles, and deal breakers. The matchmaker leverages this intel to suggest tailored matches from their pool of other clients.

Compared to online dating, matchmakers offer a more personalized touch. They get to know you deeply, allowing them to assess compatibility factors beyond surface-level profiles. Their screening, vetting, and suggestion of matches does the legwork for you.

Hiring a matchmaker tends to work best for busy professionals seeking quality connections without investing the time themselves. It also helps individuals with niche preferences or personality factors not easily searchable online.

Finding the right matchmaker starts with researching options thoroughly. Get referrals from satisfied past clients. Check credentials and community reputation. Ask about their screening process, clientele pool, and success rate for matches.

Be prepared to pay a hefty fee ranging anywhere from $500 to over $10,000 depending on service level. While not a small investment, for relationship-minded singles, the right match can be priceless.

In summary, leveraging a matchmaker allows you to outsource the search for real romantic connections to a seasoned professional. But do your homework to find one that's reputable and aligned with your relationship goals.

chapter ten

communication

Online dating revolves around texting, messaging, and emailing with potential partners before meeting in person. While convenient, solely text-based interactions have pitfalls.

Without body language and vocal cues, messages risk being misinterpreted. A sarcastic quip can read as cold over text. But a voice call clarifies tone, improving understanding. When unsure, gently check-in rather than assume intent.

Protect your personal contact details until trust builds. Many apps now allow in-app calls and video chats so you can interact safely. Once rapport develops, move to regular phone calls to gauge chemistry before meeting up.

Each generation tends to favor particular digital communication styles. Younger daters often use playful acronyms and emojis as a shorthand language. Mature singles may prefer proper punctuation and grammar. Meet in the middle by staying true to your style while trying to understand others'.

Regarding the delicate art of sexting, proceed cautiously. Sexual banter absent in-person chemistry can set unrealistic expectations. Only share what you are comfortable being potentially seen publicly. Flirty texts are exciting, but real intimacy evolves gradually.

Injecting some lighthearted emojis and GIFs shows personality beyond the written word. But overdo it and you risk seeming juvenile. The laughing face, blushing smiley, and single red rose are universally charming. Just don't rely on emojis to convey the important feelings, but use them as context to add tone like the laughing face if you tell a dry joke or send something sarcastic.

While digital communication lacks richness, with patience and care it can meaningfully connect you with others. Follow your conversational instincts while keeping your tone clear. The right matches will appreciate you for your authentic voice.

chapter eleven
boundaries

Navigating boundaries is an essential dance in dating and relationships. Fundamentally, boundaries represent our personal values, needs, and comfort levels. Respecting each other's boundaries fosters trust and positive connections.

Hard boundaries define absolute dealbreakers. Compromising these would severely violate your core being. Soft boundaries are more flexible preferences. Someone may lightly press these, allowing you to discuss and reset them.

Know your own boundaries, but also recognize that not everyone shares the exact same limits. Our backgrounds and experiences shape us uniquely. With compassion, communicate your boundaries clearly when relevant so there's no confusion.

For example, as a parent, it could be revealing too much about your children too soon. Another is getting too physically close too soon. People also have different boundaries when it comes to talking about finances.

Given that many women face safety concerns, a man insisting on her personal address early on disregards an important boundary. If unsure, kindly ask rather than assume.

Boundaries evolve as intimacy builds. Your first date may naturally warrant stricter boundaries than a trusted partner of two years. Recalibrate together as needed, but only when both parties feel respected.

While upholding your deal breakers, remain open to someone else's softer boundaries. If aerial yoga is their passion, but heights make you nauseous, perhaps observe rather than participate. These small compromises nurture lasting relationships.

With mutual care, boundaries provide healthy scaffolding for budding connections to grow. They allow us to retain our identities within togetherness. So communicate yours clearly, listen intently to your partner's limits, and align on what respects and protects you both.

chapter twelve

women vs men

Navigating dating and relationships as a man versus a woman often feels like different planets...yet we all want to find someone special. Rather than making assumptions, if we take time to understand each other's perspectives, we can avoid the stumbling blocks that are common and painful when returning to dating.

One of the most important paradigms to be aware of, is that women frequently enter dating concerned for personal safety, while for men it's the fear of rejection. Knowing this difference, women may be guarded at first, while men may come on strong. When you're empathetic and objective about these differences, then we can manage our expectations more effectively.

Whether you agree with this principle or not, it is commonly believed that women tend to prioritize partners who are dependable, emotionally intelligent, and successful. Men often favor youth and beauty first. Of course individuals vary, so look beyond stereotypes. Remember if you are looking for someone who is exceptional, always remember that the word exception implies a level of scarcity.

It's tempting to generalize negatively about others if you've been hurt. But holding resentments about an entire gender only hurts you.

Despite the challenges we may face, it's important to remember that there are still kind, genuine people out there seeking meaningful connections.

Both men and women navigating dating will encounter some who unfortunately perpetuate negative stereotypes. Just remember that many warm and compassionate individuals exist as well. Remember to approach new encounters with an open mind and heart.

Rather than generalizations and stereotypes, consider each person as an individual, and use empathy in your evaluations. Trust that your person is out there, and don't let a few disheartening experiences discourage you. Focus on manifesting the partner you dream of by leading with your own empathy, wisdom and authenticity.

Focus less on what you don't want, and get clear on your ideal partner's values, passions, and relationship needs.then seek those who meet them. Think of it as putting what you don't want in the rear view mirror, and what you do want in the direction you're driving.

Regarding attraction, we sometimes limit possibilities by traditional definitions.

This book focuses on heterosexual dynamics, because it's the only real dating experience I'm familiar with. Because of that, I would never make assumptions about the unique challenges and intricacies shaping LGBTQ+ dating journeys. I hope all readers may find useful takeaways, but encourage anyone seeking information regarding LGBTQ+ dating, to search and look for reviews on books that are tailored to your individual needs.

The truth is we all seek to love and be loved. We all want to have the feeling that fills us up and switches us on. If we lead with empathy, communicate courageously, and check assumptions, we will find meaningful connections that transcend all these complications and differences.

chapter thirteen

going on a date

Initiating the date itself takes some finesse. Traditional norms often expect men to be the pursuers when asking someone out. But some modern women will also take the lead and initiate the invite. I think because of my age, my personal experience is that women my age are more traditional and expect the man to lead everything, and for many, it's a deal breaker if you don't.

A gracious approach is to have an organic conversation where you gauge mutual interest, then propose meeting up. My best advice is to move into this as quickly and safely as possible. I have personally experienced amazing chemistry through chatting and texting and talking, but then met in person and had zero chemistry. It happens more than you think, so don't waste your time and find out sooner vs. later.

When suggesting a specific activity or venue, it shows thoughtfulness compared to a generic "want to hang out?" Just ensure you pick something aligned with their interests.

Choosing the right activity for a first date achieves a balance between comfort and creativity. Classics like meeting for coffee or drinks establish an atmosphere conducive to conversation. But creative options like mini golf, museum visits, concerts, or a cooking class give you something interactive to enjoy together while learning each other's personalities. The goal is picking something approachable without a lot of pressure associated, yet still unique enough to start strong.

Who should pick up the check?

The topic of who pays often brings debate. Some men still prefer to pick up the first date check. Others insist on splitting everything 50/50 no matter what. A thoughtful approach is that whoever initiated the date invite and venue typically offers to cover the associated costs. However, don't fight your date if they want to pay their share. You can always alternate who pays on future outings if it's going well.

Beyond logistics, nurture the date's overall tone through dress, manners, and conversation style. Avoid fixating on work talk or interrogating with rapid-fire questioning. Find a balance of listening and sharing. Express genuine interest by asking engaging questions. And put phones away to stay present. With care, the chemistry builds itself.

Body Language

Be aware that not all body language cues are reliable and try to avoid general assumptions.

Sometimes a lack of eye contact indicates dishonesty; other times, it may indicate shyness, insecurity or intimidation.

I once had a date who thought I wasn't interested because I didn't make much eye contact. I did like her, but I'm on a little on the spectrum so maintaining eye contact can be a challenge.

Another friend of mine told me that she's cold a lot and folds her arms to keep warm, but it can look stand-offish.

The art of getting dressed

When it comes to how to dress, I've always met first dates wearing casual attire and I confirm that with someone before meeting them. It takes the pressure off of that meeting, and helps everyone feel more comfortable. You can always get dressed up when it's time for something elevated.

Of course people may have different expectations, so it's always better to check in ahead of time to avoid that awkward moment when one person is casual, and the other person put in the effort. It's also a good idea to dress less provocatively on the first date. Although at times it can be a fun distraction, it might not be the attention you want from this person when you meet them in person. How you dress conveys a lot about you and your intentions. I also suggest going light on fragrances since they can be subjective and not everyone may love your cologne or perfume in high doses.

What happens after the date?

After the date, send an appreciative text or call reiterating you enjoyed their company. Based on their response and enthusiasm, you can assess mutual interest in a second date. Be sure to reflect on compatibility factors and relationship goals to determine if pursuing things further feels right. Not every great first date leads to a relationship. Trust your instincts. Do not despair if the date didn't work out. Whether it was successful or not, every date is a learning opportunity and a chance to gain perspective.

chapter fourteen
the sex talk

Deciding when you're ready for physical intimacy with a new partner is deeply personal. This is especially true if you've only been with one person for years or decades. Take time to listen to your needs and don't rush into anything you're not 100% comfortable with. Make sure you're taking this step for all the right reasons - a genuine connection, not simply loneliness or outside pressures. Check in with yourself first. Also keep in mind that sex is a wildly subjective thing and will probably be pretty different with the next person you're with.

Once you feel ready to increase intimacy, have an open discussion about affection styles and libido. It doesn't have to be as clinical as it sounds, but is a great chance to explore the topic. Some people thrive on physical touch and PDA. Others cherish acts of service or quality time. Some people have certain proclivities in regards to what they're into. Respecting each other's preferred "love languages" creates harmony. And don't compare sex drives or identities. Honor each person's unique sexuality.

When you do decide to become sexually intimate, safety should be top of mind. Always practice consent and use protection. Have an honest dialogue about recent STD testing and share verified results. The best advice if you decide to move off of protection, is to make sure you are both tested and discuss things like exclusivity, etc. Alternative relationships and lifestyles can involve multiple partners, so make sure you understand the risks you take. Don't make assumptions. Approach this conversation with facts, compassion and maturity. Your health is too important.

If you need testing or are unsure of potential risks, educate yourself thoroughly beforehand. Explore reputable online resources and ask healthcare providers.

If you have only been with one person for years or decades, the idea of being intimate with someone new can be simultaneously exciting and terrifying. Remember that your experience and their experience leading up to the moment, has probably been very different, so enter it with an open mind.

Regarding the first time together, release any pressure to be perfect. Nervousness, fumbling, laughter - embrace all the awkward joys of new discoveries. Prioritize emotional connection and exploration over impressing each other with skills or stamina. Just be present.

After intimacy, talk openly about what aspects satisfied you and what didn't. Don't critique, but communicate your unique desires. Practice aftercare by checking in on each other's emotions too. Physical intimacy should uphold your mutual care and respect.

Understand that aging impacts sex. For women, menopause affects hormones and arousal. For men, erectile dysfunction becomes more common. Have compassion. There are many solutions tailored to support your needs as individuals and a couple.

Most importantly, approach intimacy as an adventure - unknown, but inviting. Let caring for each other be the compass, even when passion falters. With playfulness, understanding and courage, your physical bond will reflect everything cherished in your emotional one.

chapter fifteen
commitments

Committing to someone emotionally comes packed with vulnerability. What dedication means to you may differ dramatically from your partner's definition. Treading with care and patience is key.

Before asking for commitment from someone else, clarify your own yearnings. Reflect on your core values, relationship objectives, and what level of dedication leaves you feeling nourished. Defining these elements first equips you to compassionately articulate desires later.

When considering exclusivity, look for signs of true availability and enthusiasm. Infatuation fluctuates, so also observe consistency between words and actions. A willing partner who reliably prioritizes you even during lows suggests genuine intention for commitment.

Timing discussions around commitment is an art, not a science. Allow trust and understanding to deepen first. When you're both organically moving in a relationship direction, share your hopes with openness and curiosity for theirs.

These poignant conversations require courage from both individuals. Avoid framing it demandingly. State your wishes, then actively listen while suspending judgment. Discover your common ground.

I got into a relationship with someone that I instantly fell in love with, even though I constantly tell people there's no such thing as love at first sight. I wanted to be open with my feelings, and although we had already discussed being exclusive, I read that as an open door to express how I was feeling. I used the "L" word. Ultimately it was too soon, and everything unraveled from there. I'm not saying the relationship would have flourished had I slowed down, but it's definitely a strong possibility and an important lesson I took away from the experience.

Outline what commitment means day-to-day in your unique scenario. How will you nurture this intentional bond as a team? Also address external factors impacting your circumstances with grace. A spirit of compromise strengthens the foundation.

While challenging, vocalizing mutual hopes around commitment can deepen intimacy and clarity. You build an enduring foundation brick by brick, together. Move slowly, communicate with care, and let your shared values guide you. And always remember that getting into a commitment should be an exciting thing for both of you.

If it's a struggle, then it is probably not the right time or even person to do this with.

chapter sixteen
ending things gracefully

Knowing when it's time to let go of a dating relationship that's run its course can be challenging. Signs like losing chemistry, emerging incompatibilities in values, or dealbreakers being uncovered, signal closure may be approaching. Reflect on whether your core needs are being met. Recognize that mutual growth, not just infatuation, nurtures lasting bonds.

If you do decide to end things, do so thoughtfully but without prolonged delay once sure. Avoid cryptic texting or ghosting, which leaves the other confused and hurt. Have an honest yet kind voice conversation explaining your feelings and decision. Thank them sincerely for the meaningful moments shared, even if brief.

When sharing your decision, aim for grace over confrontation. Rather than criticisms, use "I statements" to take ownership of why it no longer aligns for you. If they ask for specific feedback, provide it constructively but don't get into debates. Simply reiterate that your decision stands upon reflection. Equally important is to share the qualities you liked in the other person. Hearing sincere compliments can take some of the sting out of rejection. Emphasize "incompatibility" doesn't always mean someone did something wrong.

A phone call is ideal, allowing a tone discussion. Texting such news risks misinterpretation. And meeting in person presents safety concerns if emotions run high. Remember, ending relationships with care fosters your own dignity and personal growth.

After parting, process any grief, relief, or lessons learned. Then look forward with optimism. Each relationship teaches us something about ourselves and needs. Those experiences lead us closer to the thing we're looking for. Trust in your journey and embrace the unknown ahead.

I recently dated someone who was the nicest person I think I've ever met in my whole life. She was professional, smart, accomplished, gorgeous, and funny. When you meet people like that, you tend to put your best foot forward. But over time, I realized that there were areas we weren't compatible and at one point, someone noticed that I was acting differently around her, which made me realize that I was just giving her anxiety because she could tell something was wrong but didn't know what.

When I had the conversation with her, she was hurt and disappointed. But we eventually moved past it and became friends. And now when we see each other there's no hard feelings or awkwardness. That to me was probably the best possible outcome.

I've also been on the receiving end of that and know how painful it can be. You feel defeated, as if you weren't good enough. It sucks. And it doesn't go away overnight. The best advice I can give you is to pick up your normal routine and move on as best you can. Every day you'll feel a little better and eventually will be ready to get back on that horse.

In other more extreme cases, I've had situations where people turned out to be toxic, or they had a hard time letting go. That's when you need to consider blocking that person. If you're an empathetic person like I am, blocking seems very severe. But you don't do it for their benefit, you do it for your own. Also some people hang on so tightly, they would rather have a challenging back and forth with you rather than let go. Blocking can put an end to that and even help them move on sooner as well.

chapter seventeen
dealing with rejection

Rejection in dating can sting, especially after investing time in getting to know someone. The ways it manifests can vary too. Sometimes it's abrupt, like a text stating clear disinterest. Other times it's ghosting, where contact suddenly ceases altogether. Or it can be subtler, through trailing off communication or repeatedly canceling plans. Regardless, processing the emotions is essential.

Allow yourself to feel sadness, hurt, even anger - but avoid spiraling into excessive self-blame. Vent to trusted friends, but resist trash talking. And remember actions like ghosting often reflect the other person's issues more than your worthiness. Take time for self-care and activities that restore your confidence.

It's important not to take rejection personally. Two good people can still be a mismatch. You may have different visions, lifestyles, or emotional needs that make sustained compatibility challenging. Rejection doesn't diminish your value; it simply says this particular pairing probably isn't the right one for you. Don't let it internalize as a commentary on who you are, and look at it as a lesson learned and not a failure.

If asked respectfully, it's fair to receive constructive feedback as a learning opportunity for growth. But avoid debating the reasons for rejection or trying to change their mind. Once decided, pressuring your ex-partner to reconsider will only cause pain on both sides. Direct your energy into meeting new people aligned with your needs.

While painful, honor and appreciate when ex-partners are honest about their feelings fading or needing to part ways. A clean break, though difficult initially, is emotionally healthier for you both versus leading someone on or continuing an unfulfilling relationship. Allow it to redirect you towards connections embracing you wholly.

Also remember the person who is ending things may be feeling really terrible about it as well. Be empathetic to the other person who may be just as disappointed.

Though heartbreak is unavoidable, perspective and self-compassion help you move forward. Having a healthy sense of humor doesn't hurt either. In time, you'll find your enthusiasm and continue looking for your perfectly imperfect partner.

chapter eighteen
dating fatigue

The trap of over-communicating with matches is real. When juggling conversations across multiple apps with new people daily, no one gets your full attention. Meaningful connections take time and focus to cultivate. Spreading yourself too thin leads to inadvertent ghosting and shallow exchanges. Consider decreasing the inbound flow to thoughtfully nurture fewer promising prospects.

Scheduling endless first dates also takes a toll over time. The effort, planning, and expenses involved in constantly meeting new people is draining. Before moving a match from app to real life, consider vetting them more selectively. Save in-person meetings for connections showing genuine potential for compatibility.

When you've been dating extensively without any relationships blossoming, disillusionment can set in. Thoughts of "I'll never meet someone" run on a loop. But remember, connections happen on their own timeline. Take breaks when frustration builds. Have faith that the right person will arrive at the right moment.

Conversely, too many promising options can also overwhelm. Analysis paralysis sets in when you try evaluating a surplus of potential partners simultaneously. Comparison shopping people prevents giving fresh matches a real chance to shine. Go with your gut instincts when someone intrigues you.

A useful technique I created is the 30/30 rule - Spend 30 days online dating, and if you haven't met anyone meaningful by then, take 30 days off. Stepping back when feeling overwhelmed clears dating fatigue. You return renewed, avoiding burnout. The other advantage I like is that after 30 days off, there are a whole new group of people who have joined so it feels like a fresh start.

chapter nineteen
modern dating glossary

Navigating the modern dating world can sometimes feel like deciphering a new language. With the rise of digital communication and online dating, a plethora of terms have emerged to describe various dating behaviors. It's essential to understand that these definitions are fluid, and interpretations may vary based on personal experiences and cultural contexts. The following list provides a summarized version of some commonly recognized dating terms:

Benching - This involves keeping someone as a backup option while actively pursuing other romantic interests. The person on the "bench" might receive sporadic contact, just enough to keep them engaged when it's convenient.

Breadcrumbing - This is the act of sending intermittent flirty messages without genuine commitment. It's a way to string someone along, providing just enough attention to maintain a connection without real reciprocation.

Caspering - A kinder alternative to ghosting, where someone lets you down gently, explaining their intentions or feelings, before disappearing from your life.

Catfishing - This involves creating a deceptive online dating profile using fake photos and information. Often done with malicious intent, it's a breach of trust and can lead to heartbreak.

Cloaking - This occurs when someone stands you up for a planned date and then later re-initiates contact as if nothing happened. It's a form of ghosting but with a sudden reappearance.

Cookie Jarring - This involves dating someone consistently while keeping other romantic prospects on the side. It's a sign of reluctance toward commitment, as they keep options open in case the relationship ends.

Cushioning - This is the act of maintaining flirty conversations with backup potential partners. It's done to "cushion" the blow in case a seemingly promising new relationship fails.

Eclipsing - This involves adopting the interests or hobbies of the person you're dating. It's often done to appear more compatible or to strengthen the bond, even if those interests aren't genuinely shared.

Firedooring - This describes a one-sided relationship or interaction where one person always initiates contact, and the other responds only when it's convenient for them.

Fleabagging - This refers to engaging in sporadic hookups with an ex-partner after a breakup. It provides a sense of familiar intimacy without the commitment of a relationship.

Ghosting - This happens when someone suddenly cuts off all communication without any explanation. One minute they show interest, the next they vanish, leaving the other person feeling confused and hurt.

Haunting - Similar to orbiting, but with occasional interactions or likes on social media. It serves as a reminder of their presence without genuine re-engagement.

Kittenfishing - This is when someone presents themselves in an overly positive light on dating profiles. They might use outdated photos, exaggerate their achievements, or lie about their interests.

Lovebombing - This involves showering someone with excessive affection and attention in an attempt to manipulate or gain control. It's often seen at the start of a relationship and can be overwhelming.

Microcheating - Engaging in subtle actions that might skirt the boundaries of faithfulness in a committed relationship. This could include frequently messaging someone without your partner's knowledge or flirtatiously interacting with an old crush on social media.

Mosting - This is when someone displays intense affection and makes you feel incredibly special, only to ghost you shortly after, leaving you perplexed and hurt.

Orbiting - This is when an ex-partner frequently views your social media posts but avoids direct interaction. They "orbit" your world, lurking in the background, blurring relationship boundaries.

Paperclipping - This involves occasionally reaching out flirtatiously to someone, often after a long period of no contact. It's a way to keep them interested without any real commitment.

R-bombing - This is when someone reads your message but doesn't respond, leaving you in a state of digital limbo and uncertainty.

Slow Fade - This is the act of gradually reducing communication over time to end a dating relationship or interaction. Instead of directly ending the relationship, the person lets contact trail off.

Stashing - This involves hiding a new relationship from friends, family, and social media. Keeping a relationship secret suggests discomfort or uncertainty about the partner.

Submarining - This is when someone resurfaces in your life after ghosting you, without offering an explanation for their prolonged absence.

Zombieing - This is when someone who previously ghosted

you reappears in your life, often with a random message or interaction, attempting to resurrect a relationship that was previously dead.

Remember, while these terms offer a glimpse into modern dating dynamics, they're not definitive. Everyone's experiences and interpretations may differ. It's always best to communicate openly and honestly with potential partners to understand each other's perspectives and intentions.

chapter twenty
final thoughts

We've covered so much ground on the journey of dating - from building self-awareness, crafting authentic profiles, communicating thoughtfully, to moving on gracefully when a connection concludes. While the terrain brings challenges, embracing the adventure with wisdom and care unlocks rewards.

Obviously you can't remember everything in this book. The goal is to get you familiar and educated first, but provide a companion guide that you can refer to along your dating journey. If I could get you to remember five things, it would be to:

1. **Be open minded.** Release unrealistic expectations and be open to new personalities and experiences.

2. **Don't betray your instincts.** Listen to your needs and trust what your gut is telling you. Don't betray your values or boundaries.

3. **Be authentic.** The right matches will LOVE the real you. The fake you only results in fake interest.

4. **Have fun!** Approach dating with a spirit of optimism, fun, and learning. Don't let disappointments weigh you down.

5. **Communicate openly.** Communicate openly and compassionately. Seek to understand different perspectives. No one is a mind reader, so be sure the people you meet know where you're at.

There will be ups and downs, but the peaks make the valleys worthwhile. Each step leads you to self-discovery and potential partners who nourish your spirit. Savor every moment of growth.

Dating offers so many gifts beyond romantic love. You can forge new friendships, discover new passions, and improve your understanding of yourself and others. Try to celebrate each of these opportunities.

Most importantly, commit to this journey with courage, patience and care - for yourself and anyone whose path you cross, even briefly. Lead with wisdom and kindness.

The road ahead will unfold according to its own rhythm. Mind the bumps but remember they smooth in time. I wish you rich adventures, meaningful connections, and boldly going wherever your open heart leads.

Around the time of writing this book, I had started to fall in love with someone. It had all the great signs and honestly really raised the bar now for what I expect to feel like, but unfortunately it didn't work out in the end.

Although I'm going to take an appropriate break to reflect and learn, I will try again one day soon.

Thank you for reading this book. I hope you found it useful and it helped remove the anxiety of returning to dating. I also hope it gives you some objectivity and an open mind to get started with.

I'll leave you with my favorite quote of all time:

"If you want to hear God laugh,
tell him your plans"

It reminds me to always keep an open mind because that's how you discover the things that you love, that you never knew existed.

Good luck!

chapter twenty-one

about the author

I am a professional tech consultant who studied human behavior to design friendly and intuitive technology solutions for companies around the world. I grew up in Southern California but moved to Southwest Colorado where I graduated high school. After going to college in Texas, I eventually returned to Southern California and completed a 14 year career in hospitality before switching to technology consulting.

I eventually moved to the San Francisco bay area where I worked for over 20 years as a business, brand, design, and technology consultant for companies in over 15 countries.

After my divorce in 2008 I not only began online dating, but even consulted on some of the online dating services at the time. There was a time when I thought finding my person would be a numbers game and went on as many first dates as I could. Statistically it made sense, but in practicality it didn't work at all. Over the years I've been in and out of some multi-year relationships, but have learned a lot not just from my own experiences, but hearing about everyone else's.

At the time of writing this book I'm still single, but I'm always optimistic and have met some life long friends along the way. I wish you the best of luck and hope this guide helps you on your dating journey!

Made in the USA
Middletown, DE
17 October 2023